DOWN

Emma —
You are a brightness in the world!. Thank you for all you do for the literary world and in our little community here in knoxville. You rock so hard!

DOWN

poems by
Erin Elizabeth Smith

STEPHEN F. AUSTIN STATE UNIVERSITY PRESS

Please address correspondence to Permissions:

Stephen F. Austin State University Press
sfapress@sfasu.edu

ISBN: 978-1-62288-903-7
Cover art: Tristan Brewster
Managing Editor: KimberlyVerhines

CONTENTS

ACKNOWLEDGMENTS

My utmost gratitude to the following journals where poems from this collection first appeared: *Barn Owl Review*, "Něco z Alenky"; *Birmingham Poetry Review*, "Alice Dreams the Storm"; *Bluestem*, "Three Months in Tennessee"; *Cheat River Review*, "What We Undo"; *Connotation Press*, "Caterpillar and Smoke," "Alice Talks to Bonne about Love," "Alice's Sister," "Behind the Fireplace," "The Men Who Loved Alice"; *Everyday Genius*, "Dear John"; *Makeout Creek*, "Things We Do To Fill the Holes"; *Menacing Hedge*, "Alice Recounts the Unfortunate Accident with Bonne and the Rabbit," "February in Knoxville," "Alice on OKCupid"; *Mid-American Review*, "Alice in Louisiana," "Alice to Alexandra"; *Moon City Review*, "Alice in Knoxville"; *New World Writing*, "Dinah"; *North Dakota Review*, "The Secret Bodies"; Palooka, "Alice Gives Advice to Dorothy," "Alice in Kentucky," "The Carroll Illustrations," "Down"; *Reunion: the Dallas Review*, "Things I Know Just By Looking at Them"; *THEThe Poetry*, "On the Third Month of Separation"; *Tusculum Review*, "How to Get Dry," "Sesquicentennial Alice," "Alice Attends Bonne's Wedding"; *Waccamaw*, "On Dating Again"; *wherewithal*: "Alice Re-Watches Garden State"; *Zone 3*, "The Deer," "Gastronomy."

For all the Alices

&

Joe

"Down, down, down. Would the fall never come to an end?"

—*Alice in Wonderland*

.

BEGIN AT THE BEGINNING

Three Months in Tennessee

1.
It's snowing again in Knoxville.
Still the brainless daffodils open
their bright mouths to the wet.
Seven months in this globed city,
and my husband tells me
this could never be
home. I agree, though I can't
say why—I love the ravished Europa
and her lunar cow that cavort
in the square, the butter light
of our living room, high
ceilings of textured white
making shadows
of everything.

2.
A week into the season,
I think to clean the flower
beds of leaves. Beneath, small shoots
of hostas thumb through.
We amaze ourselves
with what sun and rain will do.
I can almost see them grow,
he says, as I watch the small
nameless birds peck at snails.
Nine months married and I hate
and marvel at the weight of a ring
the way its absence—in sleep,
in work, in the hot of deep
bathtubs—is a type of fear.

3.

Our chain-link neighborhood pops
with dogwood. Petals doodle lawns
like the drawings of girls
who pencil the same house,
same boxy windows
under a squinting sun.
I drew these houses once.
Now in the margins of my book
I dog-ear anything that cuts
past the single triangle tree
or the crepe myrtle,
very real,
maturing to its pink piston.

The Secret Bodies

Each year, I wear my bathing suit
all summer in the sycamore skin
between the tan. I wear it
like an innocence. The sun-touched
flesh, freckled copper, laid across
bare stomach—the raw lie of nudity.

℃

We don't always mean to hide
the memoirs of our bodies,
but we do—the flattened mole
on a heel, the Christmas-
shaped birthmark, one tiny white hair
that grows out like a horn.

℃

On my wedding ring finger
runs a thin white river
of a scar from the night
I sliced it clean on a bottle
in a drunken parking lot.
I touch it sometimes
when I slide on the band,
this memory of blood
and love, the other life
each body has.

Mapmaking

Smoking on the coffeehouse patio,
the chicken joint across the street
smells like the state-fair fry of funnel cake.
I am everywhere today—
the red and purple living room
where I burrowed in the blankets of a man
I used to love. A candy cane
rocket parked on Carolina fairground.
The orange trill of space heaters
on a Hattiesburg bar. Binghamton
where the hills doffed their autumn
and the rivers sank to barely-clothed rock.
It is almost summer in Knoxville,
the one city I haven't written yet,
still bookmarking heartache
in different states, the way
memory spins like an endless bottle
on the pavement by old houses.
Now I make love in my bed
with my husband, wearing his orange
like a New England sunset.
And it's not even Providence
I dream of, though her naked
fiery rivers still delight
and the hollowed train station
in the leaping heart of that city
is my own mole heart sometimes.
I want to chalk the greens
of Tennessee, the split seasons
tunneling into tourist shop mountain.
How it's not exactly cold here,
not like Champaign where fondant

snow iced the cars and four years ago, a man broke me
with terse car rides and fishbowls
of cheap wine. Here, maybe I can
be another woman, free of topography—
ringed, housed, given to fits
of chain-smoking and deleted history.
My life Tennessee-long
and impossibly steady,
a boat glancing off the flared
breaks in the lake. Here, I eat
the Asheville apples, galas
the size of my laced hands,
and see the limitation of road sign,
cities where others sleep in my old rooms.
Here, I poorly fold the glove compartment map,
watch with hunger as the grey squirrels
chase themselves into their trees.

Things I Know by Looking at Them

Who a person is
by how they smoke.
The brown sweetness
of cooked onion.
That pause of green
before red in jalapeño.
The way skin bubbles
from Mississippi mosquitoes
or how the pink puckered
bite longs for nails.
A perfect stirred martini.
Sunsets and weather
patterns. If a man wants
a woman in how she holds
her glass. The possibility of good
song in the dark-walled bluster
of karaoke bars. What sports
someone's played, what cities
they felt birthed from
and the miraculous bridges
that light the rivers there.
The joke you are about to tell.
The way my husband's turned
lash says whether or not
he'll touch his lips to the sleeping
crown of my head before he slips
from the sheets into the morning
where I know it is
always about to rain.

Remembering the Name
or The Ten-Month Marriage

The night he said he was leaving,
I drank everything in the house—
the freezer of vodka, two warm beers,

brandy I use for brown mushroom sauces.
I sat on the slatted wood of the deck
and tried to chart backward

with my sextant of a brimmed glass.
I thought in names, in cold beds,
in the strange alphabet of hindsight.

When he said he didn't love me,
the roof did not come off and roll
around the room, but I wanted to

knock over every table, to forget
the way my name had sounded
in his mouth, the way he'd pull

the air in between his lips
before he came. To look at his long
body on that sofa and see a foreign

thing, a stammering king
made kitten in the shaking.
Instead, the night changed nothing—

the broken flowerpot stayed split,
the door still opened at my touch,
and bottles emptied as bottles tend to do.

The Carroll Illustrations

In Carroll's drawings, Alice isn't
so proper or so blonde. Instead
a big-headed girl floundering
in pencil-quick ocean,
swimming as if holding
a tiny cup of tea.
The mouse more rat than cartoon ears,
floats like something dead
and Alice pedals past him,
plain-clothed, stone-eyed,
flicking her ankles like a seal.
No sheeted yellow hair curtsies
like a buoy on still bay.
No girlish clapped hands,
delphinium eyes singing
in the violets, but a real girl,
who is reaching
from the salted water
as if drowning in it all.

Down

for John

Five years and I keep chasing you
through tunneled earth,
without latitude or cupboards
or licking the jar
of its orange marmalade.
It's not that kind of falling.
Rather, a dream where I open
a door to the house where you live
without me. When I wake
and find myself alone
in the vast sea of my own bed,
my hands cling to the pillow
like a raft. I want to stop writing you,
to walk numb-fingered
on Champaign streets and not see
you in every turned face.

I have grown. I have eaten
and drank until I'm unsure who I am
without the slim-necked glass, lanced
olive and gin. I am no longer blue-dressed,
pinafored, a girl wrapped like a gift.
But I am still falling
through the slippery leaves,
every bit of anorexic ice,
still waking like a child roused
in the backseat, unsure where I am
in the fragile, new dark.
I sleep half afraid
of who I might find.

Behind the Fireplace

I can see all of it when I get upon a chair—all but the bit just behind the fireplace. Oh! I do so wish I could see that bit.

—Alice

The gas fire whistles in its plastic logs.
The chimney here draws nothing
but gasped heat, the blue-black
shadows of remote-control flame.

Behind it, Alice, there is little more than that—
a house mortared fifty years ago
when our small Southern city bloomed up
with snowbirds and flower-print undergrads.

Past that brick is the porch my grandmother built
to cover the concrete turned in on itself,
where my mother spun hotdogs on the grill,
smoking Virginia Slims, and I would waddle

in my blue bathing suit, young and fat
and certain the neighbors' dogs would not bite.
I have gone into the mirror, Alice.
In it, my mother blows on a cookie

fresh pulled from an oven. She runs the spigot
cold, then pours glasses of clean water,
and all the perennials we planted are up again
like painted rooks. Here my grandmother is still strong

enough to stack wood, and she lets me light
newspaper to smoke the flame. But you,

you have no father that cracks the belt
to your thigh or mother whose stomach holds

49 pills. Your sisters aren't found frothing
on the front yard at fourteen or posed, red-eyed
for the flash of police camera. The world turned
for you is made of mist and forward momentum—

it is cracked eggs and poems of boys with swords
who could never be you. Sometimes,
when I crawl through that mirror,
there is a world clean as a 50's sitcom,

but others, I am running like a rabbit
with only one hole to hide in.

The Deer

Deer have been in the garden again
clipping the heart-shaped leaves of sweet
potato, popping each tomato
before it bleeds. After the pink sky,
voracious night descends.
Raccoons pilfer eggshells, brown
artichoke, lick clean the alabaster oyster
shells and run, fat and fearless,
across the deck while deer ransack
my okra again. It's hard not to be angry
at their hunger—the green I've grown
from startled seed, earth I cultivated
as one might a room for children,
little lullabies of pinched weed and water.
This morning the soil was pitted with prints,
so I wait with a gun for the deer
with their flashlight eyes to saunter
across the lawn into my spread of summer
flowers that will blossom into squash,
beans, the heat red of pepper,
and think of my mother's garden,
crowded with inedible gourds
striped like cartoon prison pajamas.
That one season of fruiting
where she let each rot on the vine,
a decoration of perfect, hard rind
strung to the chain-link
like last year's Christmas lights.
So much like the apple tree she dug up
from my stepfather's lawn two months after
we left. Each spring it would give
such small fruit, and I would bite

through that puckering skin
to taste what she'd stolen for us.
Not at all like the muscadines I hoarded
in the wood across the street,
wild and sweet like the promise
of growing up. I was young then,
before I understood my own history
of poverty and force, before I could remember
how cold and hard a man's belt buckle
felt on the skin, the way a voice can discolor
old photographs. Before the night I saw
my mother huddled on the floor,
my stepfather's hand, the same one
she had watched him take to me,
raised like a movie's slow-motion sword.
The night I ran from both
into the woods, where the dirt and pine
hummed with spindly mosquitos. A time
when I thought deer emerging
from the sudden dark was something
of ecstasy and wonder.

What We Undo

We always color our beginnings white,
the slink of a sheet rolled in glossy
typewriter, or the squared-off canvas
we stretch to fit the wood.

We begin with a certain emptiness,
things that can be filled.
A new house beams its eggshell
walls, a church almost, or stacks
of sliced bread desperate for jam.
The party begins with rows
of empty glasses. We know the red
that colors them but the hushed gleam
is a promise more of lips,
their pink snowflake patterns,
hands that pinch the stem.

But there are no beginnings like this,
no pallid whiteness to startle to life,
no bleached sky looking for its season.
Instead a thrift store trunk, mossy doll inside.
A well-traveled box that held dishes,
then sheets. The hallways and doors
we both used to pass through.

Things We Do To Fill the Holes

Backyards, your grandmother's basil,
the blur of her air conditioning
in the New South heat. The July-ness
of June and the drag of menthols
on teeth. A chicken baking
in someone else's oven
whose temperature you do not understand.
The fabric softener smell
of new sheets. Men.
Alcohol in sneaked cups
and the synapses of new legs
against your own. The treehouse
youth of your best friend's
house and the dwindling number
on the electronic scale. Baths,
always a day away. Hands
on your exhausted shoulder,
a screamed chorus of your favorite
song. If only there was a way back
to your own bed, the one three weeks empty
from that marriage experiment
we all try—the hand first held
beneath a table at a bar in a state
you barely remember. The soggy heat
of him dampening the body,
opening something
that still cannot be filled.

On the Third Month of Separation

*"Well," Alice thought to herself. "After such a fall as this, I shall
think nothing of tumbling down-stairs!"*

In the South, sometimes heat
is the closest thing to love.
The days reduced to wet air
and fearless waterbugs. In this new
absence called separation,
I have become night-bound
with phoned voices and three-dollar
chardonnay. The first day,
I drink myself to blindness, fall
through the lighted doorway
into an empty living room.
When I wake, the bruise sails
like Australia up my thigh. I don't
want to think about fairy tales,
but I do, trained as a seal
on wet-eyed children's
promises, the cynicism
of bootstraps. But we all know,
in this world, nothing
is finished or untoothed.

Alice Re-Watches *Garden State*

What I know about moving on is nothing
like how it really works.
The movies never get it right—

there's no groundswell of viola
lighting a perfect pink ocean,
no dainty park bench to come together

to mourn, where he would probably place
his hand onto mine as a parent would.
No, in the movies there are flights

of splintered dishes but no one ever sees
the sweeping up, the shameful dustpan
that weighs in a hand like defeat.

The snotty tears that blotch the face
are not kissed away. We are taught to believe
if you run, someone will follow,

if you swaddle your sobbing
with shower curtain, steam,
someone will open a door.

But in this world, there is no final
rainy embrace. The doorknob you watch
will never turn. And no one gets off the plane.

A FABULOUS BEAST

How to Get Dry

Sometimes floods come quickly—
each slipped tear from your massive face
accumulates and you are small again,
left to boat the bitter sea. It is one way
to get through the door. The other,
demands of food and drink—
each nibbled cake, politely lipped sip,
makes you someone you are not.
Or rather, variations on a theme of you,
grown too small for your clothes again,
dress splayed on the floor like a body,
your body, forgotten in a cold sleep.
The trick is to get dry. Some think
philosophy, history's doomed carousel.
Others suggest you run—anywhere,
racing yourself until you clasp
your bony knees and forget
from where you were sprinting.
There are no towels for this
sort of rain. And it won't stop
until someone says it must.

If Alice Lived Here

To the right, Wheeling, the nail town
where Virginia splintered—bud stick
from an apple tree. Yet until today Alice didn't know
about the river, that the city juts from the shoreline
like an old man leaning from a bridge. Didn't know
    someone
could love West Virginia
the way she suddenly does.

There is so much about the Midwest she didn't know,
like those leafy greens, how she thought they were
    rutabaga or romaine.
Instead soybeans, endless rows between the corn.
Or that Illinois used to be a swamp. How the whole state
    needs
only inches of rain to grow.

ᐧ🙰ᐧ

Driving through Indiana, a city on the horizon
luminous as the northern lights.

It could be New Castle or Spicetown. She doesn't know.
Both are on the sign.

She's sad it doesn't have a nicer name, like Susanville
or Serendipity. She might be sad
she doesn't live there, because if she did,
she'd be home now thinking of someone
she loves, making pies,
in a blue room with yellow curtains.

In Delaware, Alice thinks *I could do this. I could live here.*
Buy a house with green trim. Change her name
to Lucy and sell Christmas trees by the road.
She could live anywhere—Dover. Newark. Wilmington.
She could be a Fighting Blue Hen.
She could wear the hat.

CR

And if Alice lived in Delaware, she would
tell everyone she was from Spicetown

or Susanville. She would tell them
she was a baker for thirty years,
had family in Wheeling, and a man who loved her,
who fit her body into his when they slept.

She would tell them all the little things she knew
about the country. That Columbia is the trailer park
capital of the world. That the man
on the Rhode Island state house isn't Roger Williams,
but the independent man,
the person who knows how
to plant a stake.

CR

Maybe home is a made-up place—
like love, like Wonderland. She thinks
the mountains are as photogenic
as the coast. She thinks when you travel,

you should always wear sweaters,
take pictures of yourself in the side-view mirror.

And sometimes she knows there is no place
that quiets that wailing in the skin,
the way a body knows the swiftness
of its own decay. How when her sisters
or Charlie sits next to her, but they could be anywhere.
They could be home now. And they say, *So could you.*

ॐ

She could say this was love, but she'd be lying,
though she would think it was true,
though she'd say *Let's move to Memphis,*
start a pumpkin farm. And you could call
me Lucy, sometimes,
when I whistle in the kitchen,
my hands a factory
of knuckle in the dough.

ॐ

Alice tells herself she could
raise sheep in Montana
when this doesn't work out.
Call herself Dorothy, feed
squirrels the bread she does not eat.

There she would dream
about someone who kisses her shoulder
before they fall

asleep. Suck the air in like milk
and knit scarves with yarn as grim as winter.

She would learn everything there is to know
about Billings or Helena
or Missoula.
At the rate she's going, Alice thinks,
she could be there in a day.

Alice on OKCupid

I know the way men look at me.
The long line of my legs in heels,
their flat palms pressed on an opening door.
They are too easy to find—

the counselor with his electric smokes,
that doctoral candidate with his small
town eyes, the tiny child of a med student
who still thinks martinis are James Bond cool.

I spend my nights on the front porch,
fireflies blinking in indecipherable
code. Sometimes there are men
who watch me smoke, waiting

for the bed sheets and tussle, the sweet
way they think I succumb. But there is nothing
soft left, just the damage we create
from the body, that edge of new ice

in a glass, smoke blown from a nostril
like a bull pawing at his animated dirt.
And each evaporates in the morning—
ghosts spooked by their own transparency.

The Men Who Loved Alice

It was not just you, Charlie.
The studded horseshoe pinned
to my Spanish tulle should say something
of luck, the way we hold it
late into our Victorian bloom.

Leopold was not there
when we grasped those gardenias,
yellow daisies, cut and coddled
like perfect soldiers in tight
palm. Nor were you,
though I'm sure you both
swirled some brown drink
in your mouths that night,
thinking of the bustle and fastens,
the Oxford church bells
in their hour of tongued reverie.

You could hear them everywhere—
from the pooling wet on your chessboard
to the queen's flamingoed lawn,
each tree wet with red,
a color I can't wear since you.

Later, in photographs, I am tapered
in satin collars, the dark,
close-cropped hair like nothing
you would draw me in. There was joy
in the shearing, in becoming
the thing you would not have me—
hard, deliciously obtuse

in the steely daguerreotype,
no more girl than princess
turned over and over
in the hands of men.

Něco z Alenky
or Something From Alice

In this rendition, I'm fooled
by a single knob—a drawer
of rulers and pencil filings.
Wrung like Sunday whites
and told the world made new
looks as grey as poverty and my own
dementia. Perhaps they should
put me away, like Dorothy after Oz.
Strung to the electric promise
of being a good little girl. I could
forget the wet-faced flowers
and their song, the way I'm moved,
ball-headed, from one adaptation
to the next, all by men who want
to make me nubile, blonde,
each in wonder of their new version
of my world, the one I told in the boat
to Charlie that day, the underground
network of jam and dissipating cats,
where queens rule without tantrum
or bouts of drowsy amnesia.
Where I shook the men
who thought they were kings.

Alice Gives Advice to Dorothy

Never get in a man's hot-air balloon—
he'll only ferry you to the family who opened you
to him before. There you are a child
to be tamed, turned to aprons, dustbins,
white pies cooling on windowsill.
He will take your hand and make you
something his, where in this land
you are given a crown, jeweled walkway,
a horse that flickers deliciously
from one hued gemstone to the next.
They will lose you again anyhow,
thrown to the slippery sea that opens
its maw to devour girls. What you left
to straw men and clockwork hearts
will have been changed and they will blame
the women—lazy queens,
mirrored heads of sorceresses
and you,
so foolish to believe home
is something you'd want to click your heels for,
a place where we aren't just stories
told to keep girls tight in their own beds.

Sesquicentennial Alice

A hundred and fifty years, and it's hard
to believe I'm no longer a girl,
aged into bluebonnet dresses,
spooned-up hair-do. I have become
a woman turned upside down
in behind-the-scene featurette,
all Redbox demure, gazing
with Victorian reticence
into the CVS parking lot.

How I got here, I never know,
following this cat or that dormouse
through the gardens of chatterbox
bulbs, while the CGI rabbit
flicks open his watch and proclaims
his short-hand terror no differently
than before.

Here I am adult and armored,
yet still fit in a teacup, lose
the way, wash through a keyhole
on the same feverish ebb.

Alice in Kentucky

Outside Tennessee the mountains begin
to swallow, a tongue shoveling
a story of coral, limestone
deep into the body.

Kentucky was made from this,
the winking shale turned
until it rubs fine enough to feed
the jessamine. The meadowlands
spread like a kite of green
where the rainy spring flushes
the seeds blue.

I come to Lexington to be transformed
by land, a curious hand reaching
into loose darkness. Yet there is nothing
but black in the bottom of a glass, the way
a man's fingers can shape you
in sheets. And how, suddenly naked
and grown, I grasp at my reflection
trying to crawl back in.

Alice to Alexandra

The older man has found someone younger
to photograph. Another girl slippered
like a whore, her parasol practically spinning
in sepia print. She stares into his camera

like a chimera, her witchy stockings crossed
at thin ankle. In another, she cocks
her bow above her chinned violin,
caring nothing for the closed eye stroking

of her string but rather the man
through the lens, who turned other girls into wood
block carvings, buffonted blondes
who pondered what to take

into their mouths—currant cakes, fists
of mushroom, a thin vial
commanding *Drink*. On her fainting couch,
I see her harden into a thing

more stone than child, more woman
cut apart through the legs than even the nude
girl stenciled on Victorian cards.
Before I became an acrostic myth,

a seven-year-old forever ungrown
in leather-bound editions, I held this pose
too. My ragged dress dipped below
a bony shoulder, my left hand cupped

for a beggar's purse. The eyes
unlike those closed for the kiss,
where he did not tell me to open
my mouth—but I did.

Dear John

I get it now. A decade later
as I watch the wind race leaves
down my rain-black street.

I don't want to dream you
but I do, you in that same house
always turning the knob with surprise.

There is a woman just beyond
that nostril of your door, cross-
legged on the floor looking up

at me not like I'm a rainstorm
or the phantom of the girl I was.
I don't know you now,

but I remember
you paralyzed on the blue-sheeted bed,
how I touched the flat of my palm

to your back, wondering
what hands to put on to heal,
how there is nothing in beauty

that makes up for loss, the deception
of birds, the way they sound
like memories in dusky attics.

Six months separated and you are all
I come back to, the way you would empty
into the still Champaign nights,

wondering what you saw in me,
how I must have looked like her
so perfectly young and dark-boned.

How you found me
like I look for men now, as hurt
and as clutching as you.

The Trees Full of Sound

I wait for autumn to surrender,
but it won't. Ferns still verdant
in their wet gardens, my own hands
tucking their tongued leaves.

I want to tell a different story,
one where the daffodils aren't waiting
in their own mute stupidity
to flare up again
in January white.
One where I believe
he'll never be more
than a scratched-off name
on heavy paper,
where the stacked boxes
of his things aren't
a calendar of failure.

In the growing cold, I remember
him, one thrift store table apart,
each of our hands sucked
into ourselves, the heat we brought
unsharable in the brightly-starred black,
when the world we planned
seemed like something
to be recalled, like a song on the lip
that forgets its own key.

THE MOON, AND MEMORY, AND MUCHNESS

Alice in Louisiana

Sometimes you don't need a rabbit hole,
just I-10 slipping into a city like a woman

rustling free of her jeans. Or a sheathed
straw necking up from some Everclear

daiquiri that's as green as spring
in Baton Rouge. Here, I suck venison

bones of their color and lick
each spoon given to me. It's a wonder

anything survives this appetite
for all things sumptuous. Outside

the bar, I watch the caterpillars trace
the myrtle, which opens its buds

like a nest of ants in this winter heat.
Here, they do not speak, but still seem

to blow smoke from the wet
wood, in the full dark

of some Zydeco band squeeze-boxing
as the city lounges loudly outside,

dusting off its tragedies, looking
for the next riddle to unsolve.

Alice to James Franco

It's been so easy for you, James—
your mother all educated Hollywood,
that father of yours Scrooge McDucking
his way through the mid-90s Valley.

The whole family a history of pen
to screen, Ohio art galleries
of floating world prints, then you
gifted in mathematics and beer pong.

Who's to say it's been different for me—
that drafty Oxford house where my mother
served clotted cream to the wigged deans
could have been your seaside home.

When you marry, James, I'm sure someone
will ring the bells like they did
for me, your white-laced starlet, an American breed
of royalty. Maybe I would have liked you

before the verse kicked in, before James Dean
and glad-handing Oval Office parties.
Before you slurred your webcam
inauguration. Before two hours of you

gnawing through stone became metaphor.
Before Greywolf. Before *Howl*. Before the Ivies
wooed your famous brown coif,
we could have had tea

in that hazy Wonderland of L.A.
where you would have talked
and talked about yourself and I wouldn't
have been obliged to listen.

Alice Recounts the Unfortunate Accident with Bonne and the Rabbit

When she shot into the woods
she didn't mean to kill
the rabbit. One loaded rifle
then a man said aim
into the reddish bank,
a color almost the sun
in Tennessee, or at least the way
she saw it set in sand.

Bonne held the gun to her shoulder
and the handle of it fit
like the way you try on a dress
and know. Then he told her
to pull. That slim wick
of a trigger. Just into the hill.
And she did. And the small tumble
of a rabbit fell from the trees.

She wasn't trying,
but maybe she should have
before it told us lies about time
and love, how to get
to a world more strange
and predictable than our own.

Alice, the Caterpillar, and Smoke

You weren't always bad, just another hirsute worm
buffeting in your white silk gallery. Before I was told you
were poisonous, I would pluck you from the March flash
of green, let you chart my freckled stars. I would seek you
from among the bark and rustle of my dog's chain, the bent
joints of saplings, your cryptic colors like the inching of
number two pencils. Now, lazy, man-faced, you are rolled
out on a russula, pulling on the hookah's hose, your words
pink smoke on the forests of flipbook animation. No more
a saw fly or canker worm than the blue larva the gardener
pinched up in Tennyson's colewart. The drowsy yellow-
headed worm heaped in your too-small bed waiting for time
to change you into something less ravenous. Then I too drag
deep from smoke they say will kill me—but what doesn't
anymore? Cell phones, the swerving deer, one man too
many. No different than your three-inch flip on my forearm
when I was a girl, the questions we don't answer, the way we
turn from them into the darkness of our own sleeping, not
caring who we were or who we promised to be.

Alice Talks to Bonne about Love

Sometimes momentum is strange.

You've walked into a house
that is not yours, and the baby howls
like a thing that needs cradling.

This is, maybe, how you could think of it—
want that requires wailing.

The cauldron might be filled
with soup. A woman holds
a pig like an infant, and all you want
is to sneeze.

The kitchen boils with smoke.

Then the woman says a word.
It is a violence.

You keep looking at the tabby
who grins and you don't understand
how anything can make a mouth like that.

The cook will stir the soup.
The Duchess will throw the baby
at you, screaming *This is your life
now*. It's okay if you let it go.
The child will go pink again, and hoofed,
and you'll be left only with the opening lips
of some ghostly beast, who will try
to tell you where you should go.

Dinah

At the door, Dinah has left a rabbit—
or the cleaved haunch of one and its ring
of black intestine piled daintily on the mat.
A clever trick, though not as posed
as the guillotined dove
its pert head hooped with feathers
or the perfect rodent heart
plucked from the body as a surgeon would.
There's poetry in this—the small parts
that may one day make a whole
beast, strung together like a tiny Greek
monster, a dove-headed hippogriff
bounding in timothy, just another animal
to beckon me back
and forth between dream.

Alice's Sister

What I want to be is the sister,
leaning her head on her hand, watching
the place setting of sun and thinking
of little Alice, her world filled
with sloshing mouse, tea pot
crashing against its porcelain shore.
To be the woman with girl dreams
where sleep can solve the cleaved book,
hand reaching for your unmarked thigh.
Those shepherd boys turned cats
smoldering in their grace.
Where it can all be simile—
teacups into sheepbells, a mythic
sneeze. To see the world again
as an Oxford man, where the cattle low
like promises in a field,
and the whisper of girlhood
is but a mouth of wine, a story
you knew turned bitter,
dark on the tooth.

On Waking from the Dream and Finding Nothing

I.
What we say is *Wait. Don't go.*
We make question marks of eyebrows,
beat pillows in the newly lonesome

dark. We stagger through the hallways
of our indiscretions and wonder
how they find us again, while the bedroom

fan spins callously above.
I look for chance in weather patterns,
Venus rising in neighbor trees.

I rorschach the watermarks
on walls, watch each street
for any sign of his car. I do not want

him back, but the words are returning,
swimming through my body, voices
of the dead—the white nightgowns

they were strangled in, gossamer-bright.
Tomorrow I will drive
to Kentucky where the bluegrass

is not really blue and the thoroughbreds
shake muscled bodies like flags.
What we mean to say is that we know

this cavernous place, have charcoaled its walls,
burnt black the stone with our fire.
What we mean is that we can't go back.

II.
November opens again,
to devour our sacrifice—
long-kept loves, the batting lash.

I watch it take apart the spider lilies,
their ravenous pink too tender
to bite back. Along this street maples

eye their new wardrobe, and it's impossible
not to see loss in every flippant leaf.
There are days, though,

when the singleness of a hand
on my newly scarred knee,
the Knoxville sun high in the last of its blue,

seems everything. Where the moon
in her round blue skirts, lifts
up the hem to make night

dark again, and for once, I see
no symbol in this. Just the blatant stars,
all their tender fire.

Alice Attends Bonne's Wedding

Once you lean into the hole,
there's no going back. First the fall
with its fisted jam and bric-a-brac,
your body that hit the leafy earth
with a murmured oomph.

There are no ladders tall enough—
only forward momentum, your lily stiletto
tottering toward an altar white as heat.

Someone cues Elvis on the PA, and we all hush
to see you in your sequined bustier, the practiced
up-doo cobwebbed and spun, until I cannot
recognize the woman who just last night
bubbled over in her bourbon, thinking
about the man, who now waits in his dress blues,
naked on top another woman, her long hair
spread across your pillow.

I have been here too, glitzed up and white,
gardenias clamped in wet hands,
small-stepping toward a man
I could not trust. I took his long finger,
roped it in gold, and for an instant,
I thought I'd woken, Lorina stroking
my child locks while sheep
bleated in the green.

But the story can't end that way.
Instead, you each take your flame,
see which fires the wick first.

EVERYTHING'S GOT A MORAL
(IF ONLY YOU CAN FIND IT)

Alice Ponders Knoxville

Sometimes the other side
of the glass is nothing
but Tennessee, redbuds
opening like viscera
against her interstates.
I watch the hostas
shoot their egret heads
from the green and puzzle
through the drunks
who sing a fiddled ballad
as if Dionysus himself
first strummed them
to stupor. It's April,
that witty month that breathes
like a woman grasping
her knees after the long chase.
Each lawn comes up
like a chessboard,
and I maneuver
my way through,
thinking some places
are never the Oxford homes
we grew tall in
but from the hills of the fort
those river boats could be Charlie's
and it might be my name
the grey birds call out.

On Dating Again
for Joe

I can't write love poems anymore,
the split heart

of an artichoke less pink
and full of leaves turned deadly

in their charm. Now when the stories
should begin with something

a stringed orchestra
might proclaim, I reach

into the pockets
of men who painted maps,

fables of magnolia
in Mississippi spring.

Those who made the season
long with promises

at restaurants spread
with soft-shelled mollusks,

three bourbon black cherries. Here,
in this house, you light fires

from the seasoned wood
before you put yourself

in your soft bed. The strange sea
of sheets that always waits,

while I gnaw at the evening
trying to be a woman

who knows how to make
what you call ours our own.

The High School Production

On the snowy VHS, we watch
your high school production of *Alice*,
its tiered plywood, dry ice
special effects. Here, she escapes
from pimps and dealers,
a fiercer Oliver Twist.

This was the nineties,
when I was holding the hands
of middle-school boys at the dollar
cinema and you were dating another
Erin, whose hair I imagine
in a perpetual bun.

Before all the chapter turns
and table-dancing tea parties,
before our fall and our waking,
there was always Alice,
here a high schooler
in cake paint, her Wonderland
a Nashville arts camp
where the sticky heat of teenage
boys watercolored summer.

Two years after your play,
I'd be sleeping with a man
old enough to be my father,
stealing off in cabs from parentless
rooms. And you'd be quitting college,
coming back to a house of primary color

and not knowing me
for another fifteen years.

What we did seems fated now,
each action knitted clean—
fingers linked across a table, a stranger
mixing us a drink. Different people,
like Alice, always recast and recreated,
waking from the same dream.

Alice Dreams the Storm
Hattiesburg, MS

Alice has that dream again
where the hair she plucks
from her thigh isn't a hair
at all, but the long, blue
vein she pulls and pulls
until she's afraid it will uncoil
her. In the same dream,
she's in Mississippi again.
Her ex-husband kindling
her leg in his old car. She doesn't
belong here. Even in the hazy dusk
sleep where his hand
is an awkward gym shower,
she knows the man she loves
now has just risen from their real bed
to forage for clothes
and coffee in the dark he leaves
for her. It's just sleep—
a place where history doesn't need
ambered insects to create
what was destroyed. She sits
in the dream car,
and that man makes promises
again, while she fingers
her keys, rubbing the doorknob
with a kind of reverence.
She wakes to an Instagrammed story
of that life, a city split
by the railway roar of tornado.
A thatch of memory
in a YouTube video

where the black funnel tears
down Hardy Street in the same way
she did, whiskey-drunk
with the anger she only knows
now asleep. She touches
her hand to the still-warm slip
where her man had been,
the pillows bunched
like over-stuffed bouquets,
and grasps her thigh,
where she knows,
once, she pulled
something through.

Gastronomy

Murder is commoner among cooks than members of any other profession. -W.H. Auden

That first love in Oxford —
one live oyster on a fisherman's boat.
A child palate of potato, string
cheese turned. What a cook would kill
for now—not just pepper and pig,
but flamboyantly red
marrow in Singapore stalls,
Ecuadorian goat brain that sizzles
in the cigarette dark streets.
One whole cobra—blood, bile,
its beating heart in white ramekin.

We eat and we become
something hungry.
The kabobed meat
blackening on charcoal,
the blown-glass beauty
of chocolate. The roasted
sweet of spring onion
in Spain's high sun
destroys us forever
to the too-dry chickens
of our mothers, their casseroles
of frozen broccoli, turkey cutlet.

Nothing left of us but the urge
to consume something miraculous—
stained glass sushi windows,
the snowball perfect truffle

of fresh ricotta, all those edible flowers,
nasturtium and zucchini blossom
like butterflies in sheet pasta.

If we kill, it is from desire—
the porcelain fill of bowls
with our soups, the want
of something we can hold
to our lips, in our mouths,
and devour.

The Dormouse Dreams

It's always six o'clock now,
the grey hour when the pines
flicker in a black madness
of wind. That almost hour
where the kitchen is not yet alive
with onion skin and cutlery
but light bleeds along the ridge
and hares huddle in warrens.

When you are home but parked
in the flashing monitor dark,
I pace between rooms deciding
where to be sedentary.
It's not tea-time in Tennessee,
though I could set the table
with biscuits and warm chamomile,
could riddle endlessly
about where we go in the bright
hours when the slippery sun
sets itself defiantly in the sky.

Before I go mad again,
slip your fingers in
my soft clothes, unbutton
this restless dusk
until the day quickens to star.

The Last Snow

The last snow pants in the milky dawn,
unable to stay anywhere but afloat,
while the daffodils have curled back
to their fleshy bulbs.
The rest of winter stuck on loop—
apricot blossoms, white as storm,
shiver on their boughs.

On each country drive, she waits to see
the triage of redbud, the dainty dogwood
littering bloom. Hopes the hills blush
a Paris green, but instead the lake
is drained again, bluegills gasping
on its ruddy shore. Even home is not a place
for early ramps and spring peaches. There,
her tiny wrists vibrate in the draft left
by the thick quiet without birds.

Alice don't know what this reminds her of,
but she's old enough to understand
the split space of grey, how winter creeps
back just when we believe in warmth again.

February in Knoxville

The lawn finally goes brown
with a dusting of leaves and turned earth.
The stalks of daffodils invert
and the purple husks of berries
hang like baskets from their vines.

February, and there's no more snow,
just the showy wind making everything
crackle. Still, the city blinks in blue
and white, its people wrapped
liked crunchy gifts. I breathe
into cupped palms, walk the streets
that turn into others, and watch
as the sun kicks light
off our city's strange sphere.

We cannot choose where we love—
a place picks us from the flyaway
denizens who root and seed,
from the boxes that open
and reseal with no hands to lift them.

Sometimes we empty and are never
filled. Sometimes the rosemary
lasts through winter and mint comes
back like a hero on her masted ship.
And sometimes the sweetness
of cities and seasons is enough
to clean the body of its harm,
and we must take what lives to the lips,
to see if maybe,
maybe it can heal us again.

THANK YOU

Thank you to all of the people who helped bring this collection, finally, to print, particularly Sara Henning and Jasmine An who helped me to find the heart of Alice, and Kimberly Verhines and the fine folks at Stephen F. Austin State University Press for believing in the work.

To my workshop friends—too many to name, but you know who you are—who gave me their time and insight on these poems along with beer and nacho cheese stains.

To Emilia Phillips and Amorak Huey who took the time the time to write thoughtful and generous blurbs.

To the University of Tennessee Hodges Fund, which allowed me the time and space to finish this collection

And finally to Joe Minarick, who supports me every day in this weird and wonderful world. You made this book have a happier ending.

Erin Elizabeth Smith is the Creative Director at the Sundress Academy for the Arts and the Managing Editor of Sundress Publications. She is the author of two previous full-length collections, *The Naming of Strays* (Gold Wake, 2011) and *The Fear of Being Found* (Three Candles, 2007).

Smith is the editor of two anthologies, *Political Punch: Contemporary Poems on the Politics of Identity* and *Not Somewhere Else But Here: Contemporary Poems on Women and Place,* and her poems have appeared in numerous journals, including *Ecotone, Guernica, Mid-American, Crab Orchard Review, Cimarron Review,* and *Willow Springs,* among others.

She holds a PhD in Creative Writing from the Center for Writers at the University of Southern Mississippi and is a Distinguished Lecturer at the University of Tennessee where she teaches creative writing and literature. In 2017, Erin Elizabeth Smith was inducted into the East Tennessee Writers Hall of Fame.

CPSIA information can be obtained
at www.ICGtesting.com
Printed in the USA
JSHW050709161020
8787JS00001B/12